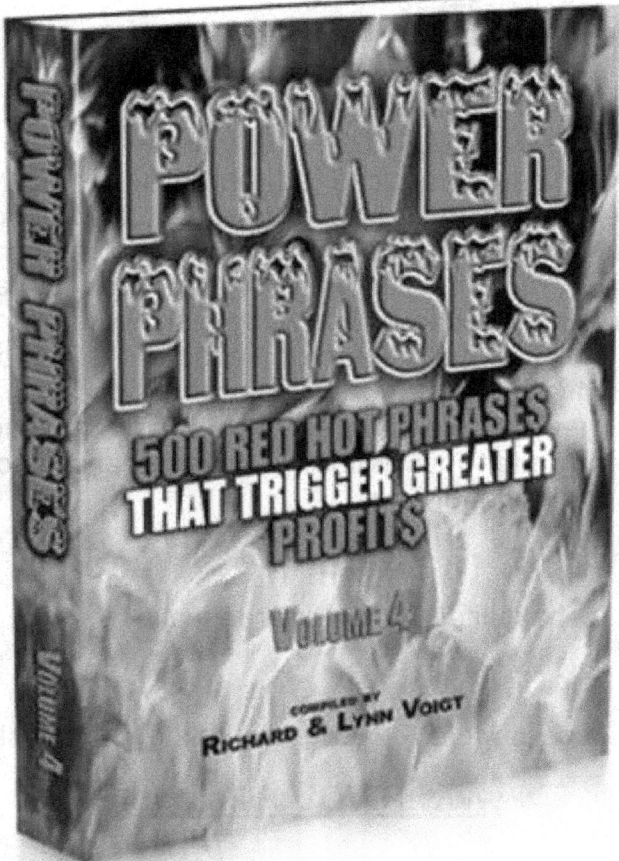

POWER PHRASES – Vol. 4
500 Power Phrases That Trigger Greater Profits

ISBN-13: 978-1-940961-04-0
ISBN-10: 1940961041

First Printing, 2013

Printed in the United States of America

To Access More Powerful Marketing Tools Visit:

www.RIVObooks.com

www.RIVOinc.com

www.WisconsinGarden.com

Income Disclaimer

This book contains educational materials meant to inspire ways to promote personal ideas, products and services that may be appropriate to incorporate or use in one's personal or business strategy, marketing method or any other related personal or business, that regardless of the author's results and experience, may not produce the same results (or any results) for you. The authors make absolutely no guarantee, either expressed or implied, that by implementing any ideas herein will gain success, make money, or improve current personal or business circumstances. There are simply far too many variable factors that come into play regarding any level of achievement or success in said personal and/or business venture. Primarily, results will depend on the nature of the product or business model, the conditions of the marketplace, the experience of the individual, and situations and elements that are beyond your control or that of the authors.

As with any business endeavor, you assume all risk related to investment and money based on your own discretion and at your own potential expense. If you intend to quote, copy, or use any content herein, in part or whole, it shall be the sole responsibility of the individual to be mindful of all active and lawfully protected copyrights, trademarks, and/or services-marks, by conducting due diligence prior to said usage.

Liability Disclaimer

This book is strictly intended for educational purposes only and was intended to inspire the individual to create ideas of their own design. This book represents the views of the authors as of the date of publication. Due to constant changing conditions facing the information age, the authors reserve the irrevocable right to modify and update their opinions based upon changing conditions. While the authors have made a "good faith" effort to verify the accuracy of information within this book, the authors or their affiliates/partners do not assume any liability or responsibility for inadvertent errors, omissions, or inaccuracies. This book is not intended to be used as a legal guide or resource, nor are the authors attempting to render any legal, accounting, theraputic, medical, or other professional services or advice. If said professional consultation or adivce is required, the authors recommend the reader immediately seek the services of a competent professional. It shall be the reader's responsibility to be fully aware of any and all federal, state, local or country laws that govern and/or affect personal or business transactions. Any slight of ethnicity, culture, gender, orientation, or existing organization as is any reference to persons or businesses, living or dead, is unintentional and purely coincidental.

Terms of Use

You are given a non-transferable, "personal use" license to this book. You cannot distribute it or share it with other individuals. Also, there are no resale rights or private label rights granted when purchasing this book. In other words, it's for your own personal use only.

POWER

PHRASES

Volume 4

500 POWER PHRASES THAT TRIGGER GREATER PROFITS

_-·|·_-•·*″‴*·•·_-·|·_-•**•_·|·_-•·*‴‴*·•_·|·_

Compiled by

Richard & Lynn Voigt

I.M. Education Specialists

Introduction:

Powerful Phrases, Headlines, Sub Headlines, Slogans, Bullet Points and Interview Sound Bites are perhaps the most powerful marketing tools mankind has ever created. They are the lifeblood behind every business venture are the ultimate secret weapon of Millionaire Marketers.

No matter whether you are introducing or promoting a brand new product, teaching a "How To" skill, building a website, or simply sending an email, using the perfect power phrase is crucial to capturing and holding eyeballs and producing greater marketing profits.

In today's world every word you use has measurable impact. Each word can produce emotional psychological buttons that trigger psychological reactions. Successful advertisers understand that using an effective power phrase is a true art form that turns "wants" into instant gratification "needs." Once artfully triggered, any niche market can instantly create more protifable conversions.

Now it's your turn to personalize this incredible collection of 500 Power Phrases in ways that instantly advance your own effective marketing skills as you create new and power phrases, slogans, presentations, bullet points, or interview sound bites that take you to the next level.

Whether starting or running a small business, writing an ad, coming up with a memorable slogan, making a major corporate presentation, bullet points, creating a video, writing a book, searching for the perfect slogan, teaching a lesson or book report, your creative use of these Power Phrases can capture more eyeballs and produce some amazing rewards quickly turning you into a Marketing Genius. Now, it's your turn to make the magic happen!

POWER PHRASES

Volume 4 – 1501 - 2000

500 Power Phrases That Trigger Greater Profits

Begin Selecting & Customizing Your Perfect Marketing Phrase

1501	Can't Can't Can't
1502	Are You Really Excited
1503	Why Reinvent - Just Improve
1504	Working At Home Without A Stubborn Boss
1505	Business As Usual Is Dead
1506	For People Who Never Start
1507	Optimize Your Efforts
1508	Classified Ad Sites That You Can Post Too
1509	No Standard Procedure
1510	The Real Big Secret
1511	Protect Your Software And eBooks
1512	Meet Your Match And Save
1513	People To Watch
1514	The Email That Changed My Life
1515	Exact Art Of Generating Unstoppable Income
1516	I Want You To Get Started Right Now
1517	Work Whenever You Want To
1518	Fulfill A Fantasy
1519	Getting Your Site Into The Hands Of Search Engines
1520	It's In Your Pocket
1521	Top 101 Tips Of The Day

1522	Remember Everything Is A Test
1523	Be Generous With Yourself
1524	Make A Case For The Product
1525	Identify Solutions To One Problem
1526	Stop Learning
1527	Consider This As A Blend
1528	All About My Early Failures
1529	Write Down The Daily Things You Want To Accomplish
1530	One Giant Event
1531	One Heck Of A Ride
1532	Hire A Robot To Make Your Sales
1533	I'm Back From Paradise
1534	Earn A Residual Profit For Life In Minutes
1535	Why Can't Everything Be So Easy
1536	Your New Career Is Calling
1537	Remarkable Point And Click
1538	Black and White Photos That Will Amaze Your Mind
1539	I Couldn't Wait To Get My Hands On These
1540	Contact Thousands Worldwide
1541	Honest Clear And Direct Marketing Techniques
1542	Scams Rip-Offs Hype And Half Truths
1543	Why You Need To Act Now
1544	Adapt It To Your Situation
1545	For Those Who Think You Can't
1546	Video Mobile
1547	Profit From Your Subscribers From The Moment They Sign Up
1548	The Real Value Of Money Time And Work
1549	How To Write So People Buy
1550	Unmatched In History
1551	Secrets Of Making Money
1552	One Thing At A Time
1553	Don't Over Complicate It
1554	Sell Only Things You Believe In That Work
1555	Get Into My Head And Under My Skin
1556	Letting Yourself Down
1557	New Way To Manage Your Game
1558	Only 10% Above Wholesale/Dealers Cost
1559	What Would You Like For Free

1560	This Is Too Important To Miss
1561	Stay The Course
1562	Is Competition Killing Your Affiliate Commissions
1563	Offers To Put On Your Buy Buttons
1564	No Connections No Skills
1565	Doesn't Require A Big Shift In Your Approach
1566	You Don't Have Space To Waste
1567	Start Talking With Your Prospective Customers
1568	How Much Money Can Be Made From This Activity
1569	Do Your Customers Know What They Want
1570	Your Newest Top Dollar Client
1571	Two Weeks To Success
1572	A No Nonsense No Obligation Approach
1573	No One What To Go Crazy
1574	The Niche Giveaway
1575	Deep Marketing Dive
1576	Leveraging Existing Stuff You Already Have
1577	Sure Fire Way To Get Ahead
1578	Did Their Headline Catch Your Eye
1579	Targeted So Well They Can't Help But Buy
1580	Still Pounding The Job Pavement
1581	Favors Have A Shelf Life
1582	But That Early Anticipation And Excitement Soon Dies Down
1583	Eliminating The Risk Of Loss
1584	Easy Payment Plan
1585	Supportive Social Networking
1586	Monetize Your Own Hot Content Ideas
1587	Looking For A Talented Team Working For You
1588	Huge Marketing Error
1589	Always Convey Your Principal Sales Point
1590	Experience Financial Freedom
1591	Grease The Pat To Excellence
1592	Explosive Revenue Campaigns
1593	Wholesale Video Game Sources
1594	Summer Into Wisconsin
1595	More Than Ever Thought Possible
1596	Gate Keepers Or Star Makers
1597	Three Word Style Statement

1598	Digital Bananas Forever Isn't A Slippery Adventure
1599	Reenter Your Request
1600	It's Bigger Than You
1601	My Top Plan Of Attack
1602	Here's Your Chance To Personally Meet Some Amazing Entrepreneurs
1603	Learn A Lot From This Approach
1604	Marketing Conversions Begin On Page One
1605	Answering Questions In A Timely Manner
1606	Anything You Want
1607	Taking Charge In A Struggling Economy
1608	Spring Marketing Catalog
1609	Quite Trying To Impress Your Audience
1610	Learning Stuff The Hard Way
1611	Make Money Tonight
1612	Don't Miss This Next Session
1613	Here Are The Important Questions To Always Ask
1614	Making Money The Easy Way
1615	Know The Business From Top To Bottom
1616	Place These Tasty Web Sites On Your Menu
1617	iAd Apple Mobile Ad Platform
1618	The Only Difference Between These Two Are Attitude
1619	Target All Your Niche Learners
1620	Mindsets Change Quickly With An Effective Coach
1621	It's Kind Of Just What We Do
1622	Information On Demand
1623	Start Unflattering Your Mind
1624	Bring On The Affiliates
1625	Fools Like To Complicate Simplicity
1626	Share Your Experiences To Draw People Closer Together
1627	Simplifying The Complex
1628	Watch The Magic Numbers Start Flying In
1629	Your Level Of Presence
1630	Pure Positive Energy
1631	Maybe You Won't Want To Go To Bed Just Yet
1632	Turnkey Domains For Sale Website
1633	More Likely To Happen Now
1634	True Or False - You Have Enough Money

1635	The Reason We Do This
1636	Create Killer Landing Pages
1637	Why 95% Go Bust
1638	Join The Team
1639	Want More Traffic
1640	The Problem They Are Trying To Solve
1641	Turning A Profit From Home 24/7
1642	Success Starts With Something Of Value
1643	Avoid Inner Conflict In Both
1644	Get A Freebie Just For You!
1645	Can You See Yourself Doing This
1646	It's Time To Make The Offer
1647	Elite Coaches And Mentors From Around The World
1648	Blow Conversion Rates Out Of The Water
1649	See Who Clicks
1650	Do The Math On The Results
1651	Avoiding High Risk Burn Out
1652	Category Selling
1653	Give Others A Chance To Deliver Ideas
1654	Why Do You Continue To Ignore Your Niche
1655	Love Your Body Language
1656	Focus Your Question On One Specific Subject
1657	Infamous Butterfly Ballot
1658	Ways To Propel Visitors To Your Order Page
1659	I Want To Make This As Simple As Possible
1660	Give Them Specific Directions
1661	Have An Instant Video Business
1662	Let's Seal The Deal
1663	Key Is How Serious Are You
1664	Get Something Extra
1665	No Story No Sale
1666	Engage Customer's Interest Longer
1667	Illusive Link
1668	Set Up Your Order Taking
1669	Category Copywriting
1670	Wealth Freedom And Success
1671	Do You Know What They Want
1672	Sold Out Within One Hour

1673	Looking For A Money Miracle
1674	Guarding Your Paycheck Keywords
1675	What's Your Million Dollar Plan
1676	Care To Join Us
1677	In Case It Wasn't Obvious
1678	What You'll Learn Once You Retire
1679	Make Money With Each Blink Of Your Eye
1680	Logic Is Only Based Upon Theoretical Prevention
1681	Stop Working So Hard Trying To Capture Traffic
1682	The Target Just Got Bigger
1683	Want A Free $500 Audit
1684	A Product that People Actually Need
1685	How Courage Gives You Power
1686	4 Easy Steps
1687	Need A Photo Restored
1688	You Deserve To Know This As An Investment In Yourself
1689	Watch Your Earnings Skyrocket As You Learn
1690	You Know You Need Sub Headlines Tools
1691	Facebook Allows You To Build Lists
1692	Really Stupid Ideas
1693	Do You Clothes Date Your Video
1694	Seek Self-Promotion
1695	Making A Good Faith Effort
1696	Time To Tell The Truth
1697	Ask For Help
1698	The Age Of Pain Is Gone
1699	What's Your Unknown Story
1700	Become An Independent Advocate
1701	Sale Of The Millennium
1702	Five Easy Ways To Make Money From Your Blog
1703	FEAR Is A Dream Killer
1704	Google Translation; Translating Web Pages
1705	Makes My Job A Lot Of Fun
1706	Create A Position Hook
1707	Software Tells All
1708	Get Rich In Your Niche
1709	Predicting Search Volume
1710	I'm Not A Blind Beast

11

1711	Fast Action Rewards Bonuses For Decisive Members
1712	Let Me Put You At Ease
1713	Find The Time
1714	Active Imaginations Wanted
1715	They Will Buy Bundles
1716	Is Your Head Still Spinning
1717	All We Have Is Our Minds
1718	I Have A Direct Line To The Creator
1719	The I-tis Trap
1720	Working Without A Plan Is Doomed To Breed Failure
1721	Is Your Life Becoming A Soap Opera
1722	Quick Easy And Free To Use
1723	You Deserve A Real Opportunity To Enjoy Your New Profits
1724	Build A Habit
1725	Love Your Offer
1726	The Key To Creating Headlines That Prospects Love
1727	Well Now You Can
1728	Distinct Immediate And On Going Solutions
1729	Come To The Garden With Your Shovel
1730	Giving To Those Who Need It The Most
1731	Sport Of The Ages
1732	Want To Push People's Buttons
1733	Simplicity Always Sells
1734	Change The Way You Think About Doing Business
1735	Get To Know And Love Characters
1736	You Want Them To Look At Your Face
1737	No Idea What To Do Next
1738	Maybe You're Not Tracking Well Enough
1739	Yes It's Here
1740	Wistful Tones
1741	Seriously Dude - It Just Doesn't Sleep
1742	I've Worked With Many Of Them
1743	The Advances Of Being Smaller
1744	Flashbacks On Success
1745	Use This Secret Responsibly
1746	Lead With One Close With One
1747	Digital Heaven On Earth Is Yours For The Taking
1748	Tie It Into Urgency And Scarcity

1749	Making The Right Move
1750	Create Unlimited Categories And Subcategories
1751	Make Windows XP Shut Down Faster
1752	What Everybody Ought To Know About This Business
1753	Think About It
1754	Automatically Incorporated Into This System
1755	Free To Find Out
1756	These Will Not Make You Rich
1757	Support Vendors Waiting To Become Affiliates
1758	How About A 5 Day Trial On Us
1759	Get It Listed For Free
1760	Don't You Deserve To Be Next
1761	Comes With A Full 100% Guarantee
1762	Website Design Keys That Help You Sell
1763	The End Result Is Worth It
1764	The Impact It Deserves
1765	Why Quibble
1766	This Is Not A JOB
1767	Not Bad At All
1768	Concepts Tested And Proven
1769	How Much More Productive Are You
1770	Do You Know What Really Excites Me About This
1771	Will They Stop And Read
1772	A Handful Of Trusted Friends
1773	There's No Reason Why It Shouldn't Be You
1774	What We Do Is Sell Them What They Want
1775	Your Marketing Solution
1776	Survey Their Wants And Needs
1777	Here's Your Assignment For The Week
1778	Trying And Still Failing
1779	Is Your Work Very Intense
1780	29 Easy Web Design Tricks
1781	A Direct Challenge
1782	How About Brainstorming This One
1783	Use Red Paint In Section 17
1784	If You Order Now You'll Receive Everything Listed Below
1785	Becoming A Great Manager
1786	What Highly Innovative People Seek

13

1787	Make Your Spouse And Your Kids Happy
1788	Failure To Probe
1789	Profitable Shortcuts To Sustainable Online Business
1790	Are You Working Yourself To Death
1791	Unconditional Traffic
1792	Want More Time For Enormous Wealth Fun And Excitement
1793	Build Your Own Information System
1794	Free Shopping Genie
1795	Requires One Simple Thing called ACTION
1796	New Travel Benefits Included
1797	You're Now The Bank
1798	You've Got Me Live One On One
1799	Encourage Others To Innovate For You
1800	Dress Your Website For Success
1801	Test Your Website Now
1802	More Buy Buttons More Profit
1803	Years Ahead Of The Competition
1804	Create Your Own High Ticket eClass
1805	Just Announced For The Very First Time
1806	Analyzing Customer Data For Clues
1807	Did You Forget Your Own List
1808	Building Better Brains
1809	Now Reason To Be Anxious
1810	Charge 1/10 Of Your Price
1811	Internet Marketing Integration
1812	Providing Simplicity And Precision
1813	100 Percent Financing
1814	How Much Rejection Can You Take
1815	Offer Them A Decision
1816	Isn't It Time You Turned Things Around
1817	Real Truth About Multiple Income Streams
1818	Create Lasting Evergreen Income
1819	The Fastest Way To Making Millions
1820	Work For Yourself
1821	Without A Huge Payoff Why Bother
1822	There's Got To Be A Better Way
1823	Top Minds Think Alike
1824	Give Value Before You Sell

1825	Front Row Seat To Your Own Success
1826	Implement My System
1827	Speak With Empathy
1828	Wage Your War Against Fear
1829	I Couldn't Take It Anymore
1830	May I Send You A Free Gift
1831	Begging For A Solution To What You Really Want
1832	Make The Cash You Deserve
1833	Going Broke Was The Greatest Day Of My Life
1834	Stop And Do It Now
1835	Good That We Found You At Last
1836	Never Forget About Your Customers
1837	Seal Of Approval
1838	A Simple But Powerful Web Site
1839	Headlines Are Scary If Not Memorable
1840	Why Minds Attempt Deception
1841	Ad Campaign That Makes Huge Money
1842	Score Real Savings
1843	Pass The Look Test
1844	Drink Lots Of Water
1845	Increases Innovation And Production Methods
1846	I Had No Idea Of What I Was Doing
1847	Laying The Groundwork
1848	But That's Not You, Right
1849	This Market Is Truly Massive
1850	Online Marketing Screener
1851	100% Of Our Members Make Money
1852	Wise Choice Wise Decision
1853	Who Said Size Doesn't Matter
1854	Make Them Feel Great
1855	Do The Walk Around
1856	Give Your Joint Venture Offer An Extra Punch
1857	I've Really Got Your Number
1858	Jealousy Envy And Pain
1859	Products Which Produce The Most Money
1860	What's The Cycle Of Your Website Visitors
1861	Selected And Complied Just For You
1862	Why Does This Make Me Money

1863	Grab Their Subconscious Mind First
1864	Boldly Coming To Your Aid
1865	When You Focus On A Goal Measurement Will Be Powerful
1866	Zombie-Killing Tactic
1867	Lost Key Retrieval
1868	Internet Marketer Hit By Headline
1869	Trying To Figure It All Out Sucks
1870	Investing In Niches
1871	When A No Becomes Yes
1872	Are Zombies Killing Your Profits
1873	Help Us Build A Virtual Village
1874	You Can Just Copy What They Did
1875	Clean Freak
1876	A Successful Turnaround Depends On You
1877	A Fairytale Business
1878	It's Time To Get The Whole Story
1879	Master The Millionaire Language
1880	I Have This Spreadsheet
1881	Specific Patterns That Create Success
1882	Let Me Show You How For Free
1883	Stimulate Your Brain With Fun Time
1884	Instantly Create Massive Waves Of Free Traffic
1885	Take Advantage Regardless Of Your Circumstances
1886	You And I Have A Lot In Common
1887	You Have A Right To Be Heard
1888	Marketing Deliverables
1889	Some Secret Success Sauce
1890	When Two Souls Unite It's Magical
1891	Praised For Our Marketing Innovations
1892	Santa Wanted Christmas To Coming Early
1893	Mesmerizing Sales Presentations
1894	Sorry Boss But You're Fired
1895	Please Note - The Master Is In
1896	When Did Your World Begin
1897	Why Didn't You Market Today
1898	Take Your Time
1899	Free Trial
1900	Hot Products

16

1901	Experience The Power Of Marketing
1902	Stories Sell Stuff
1903	You Get Over $1200 In Bonuses
1904	My Step-By-Step Screen Shots
1905	Take Fear Out Of Buying
1906	Bite The Silver Bullet
1907	Are You A Big Believer
1908	Building Influence With Free Membership Sites
1909	Google Chrome Installation
1910	Make A Realistic Plan Of Action To Follow
1911	Winter Sale Now Heating Up
1912	Ultimate Source Of BUZZ Leverage
1913	No Cost Resource
1914	Your Current Predicament
1915	Setup A Squidoo Lens That Helps Bring In Money
1916	So Powerful You Think You're Cheating
1917	What If You Could Find The Perfect Prospects
1918	Members Pay You Money Just To Join For Free Today
1919	Find Locate And Acquire
1920	Time To Make It Rain
1921	Always Pay Yourself First The Bills Will Still Be There
1922	Hold Your Breath For A Moment
1923	Networking Like The Pros
1924	Why There's Scarcity Of Profits
1925	Don't Cheat Yourself Treat Yourself Instead
1926	Here's The System In A Nutshell
1927	Use This And You'll Be Unbeatable
1928	Draw People In With
1929	I Teach By Doing
1930	Aren't You Glad You Asked
1931	Thoughts That Destruct
1932	Make Sure You Open This Web Page
1933	Marketing Co-Worker Needed
1934	No Hassles Refund
1935	Young Ones Like New Ideas
1936	Forget Stuffy DVDs And Home-Made Videos
1937	Sometimes The Lead Story Doesn't Make The Headlines
1938	Delivered Directly To Your Desktop

1939	Higher Archive Of Needs
1940	Don't Stand On The Sidelines
1941	One Of A Kind Program
1942	Are You Really Prepared To Handle A Flood Of Orders
1943	See A Whole New Perspective On Effective Marketing
1944	It Really Simplified Success
1945	Don't Forget One Time Money Offers
1946	Get Your Hit Counter Spinning
1947	IMPORTANT: READ THIS NOW
1948	Most People Fail To Grab The Opportunity
1949	Survey vs. Focus Group
1950	Don't Go Into Business Until You Memorize Them
1951	Hit Them At The Hot Point
1952	Here's The Scoop
1953	But Wait Till You Hear This
1954	Make Money Today - Get Started Now
1955	Know What You're Getting Into
1956	In Fact It's Downright Simple
1957	Take The First Step Toward Your Dream
1958	Ways To Earn Extra Money
1959	Piracy Is Free Advertising
1960	If There's A Money Back Guarantee More Sales Occur
1961	Transmit That Recognition
1962	Classic Polished Edge
1963	Meet The New Boy In Town
1964	I've Just Sweetened This Deal Big Time
1965	Internet Explorer Market Share
1966	This Ain't Chump Change
1967	Putting In The Time And Effort
1968	I Have A Marketing Riddle For You
1969	You Ever Felt CONFUSED
1970	You Really Don't Want To Get This Wrong
1971	Hating To Lose
1972	Much More Than Meets The Eye
1973	Making Stuff Faster
1974	Uncover Profitable Markets Not Yet Recognized
1975	Offer Ends Soon
1976	Certainly Gets People's Interest

18

1977	Never Be Afraid Of Failure
1978	We Hate Negative Thinking
1979	No More Worries
1980	Products You Want With Links
1981	As We Speak Email Is Dying
1982	Not So Flattering Nickname
1983	Powerful Component #3
1984	The Internet Is All About Advertising
1985	These Psychological Triggers Make People Buy
1986	Want To Expose Your Website
1987	Want To Be A Money Guide
1988	Avoid Loud Patterns
1989	So Why Do I Go Deep Like This
1990	Your Message Arrives In Only Seconds
1991	Learn To Fight Back
1992	Can't Sit And Watch Anymore
1993	Yours For Free Right Now
1994	Wouldn't You Like It Now
1995	Huge Well Defined Dreams
1996	Get Started On The New Path To Life
1997	Not Many Know About This
1998	I Want To Spoil You
1999	Testing An Idea Is Crucial To Fine Tuning Results
2000	Are You Insane A Lifetime Money Back Guarantee

Lynn and I hope that this "Think Tank" volume series of 500 Hot Phrases will helped you clearly paint your dreams, sell your ideas, and market your messages, propelling each of your ideas and projects toward incredible success. Watch for our next Volume!

We truly wish you the very best and look forward to hearing your success stories.

Concluding Thoughts:

Ever success is built upon a preparing a strong foundation, having a clear vision, and taking positive action each and every day. If you've been searching for a new lifestyle, then you'll find this book directive and inspirational. You can open it to any page and let that page help you rethink possibilities, consider new ideas, open new opportunities, and ultimately experience a more successful and fulfilling lifestyle.

Every problem has a solution! Regardless of your current situation or circumstance, know that you have the power and responsibility to redirect your life in any direction you choose. Simply start thinking about and research the kind of lifestyle that truly appeals to your heart. Begin your new journey by learning everything you can about your chosen subject. When you make that commitment, you'll open more unexpected doors to unique opportunities than imagined.

"Creative Thought Is The Only Reality
Everything Else Is Merely The By-Product Of That Thought."
- Walter Russell

So why not start thinking **BIGGER? It won't cost you any more.** It all starts by never allowing your current life's situation, environment, or so-called friends to limit your path to a happier, healthier, and successful life. After all, whose life is this?

Make a decision to focus on learning something new each and every day. Begin attracting your ideal lifestyle by doing something you love and enjoy. As difficult as it may be, don't allow money to limit your dreams. Focus on the kind of thoughts that make you feel good. Once you learn how to control your focus, you'll have a great chance to see your dreams take shape. You've finally learn to harness the power you always had within, a Universal Energy stream that flows 365/24/7 in any direction your project your thoughts, Good or Bad. Want proof? The thoughts you currently believe and project reflect the life you're currently living. Therefore, if your life isn't happening, change your thoughts, and change your life. It's something only you can hold, visualize, and project, living your dream come true.

Find yourself a mentor and spend more time with people who truly appreciate, support, and foster your dreams. Life may be short, but the thoughts we hold can make our life wider and more fulfilling.

20

About The Authors:

Richard and Lynn develop creative strategies that paint dreams, sell ideas, & market messages   Together, they present a unique team-approach, working side-by-side, helping clients pursue their passions while sharing their skills and diverse expertise as authors, artists, inventors, entrepreneurs, & Internet marketing education specialists.

Teaching by example, they mentor proven self-publishing services, graphic design, video production, domain acquisition, and marketing research of behalf of their company, RIVO Inc – RIVO Marketing, since 1997. They've created & produced hundreds of videos, self-published dozens of books on a wide variety of topics and created thousands of original works of fine art, while refining their Internet Marketing techniques, mentoring programs, and related business website development.

Their mission is to continually uncover new products and services, test new strategies, and network useful solutions with off and online entrepreneurs, small business owners, writers, local artists, models, teachers, students, and marketing professionals.

Their goal is to help clients create an action plan that discovers and connects the missing pieces of the success puzzle. The goals they foster create multiple streams of income for today's volatile economic climate. Their motto is: "Do the work once and allow the work to create additional streams of income for a lifetime."

Feel free to contact them if you have questions or would like to tap into their talents and expertise. They appreciate your feedback and look forward to hearing your success stories.

Contact:
Richard & Lynn Voigt - RIVO
I. M. Education Specialists

RIVO INC - RIVO Marketing
13720 West Keefe Avenue
Brookfield, Wisconsin 53005 – USA
Email: support@RIVOinc.com
Website: www.RIVObooks.com
Website: www.WisconsinGarden.com

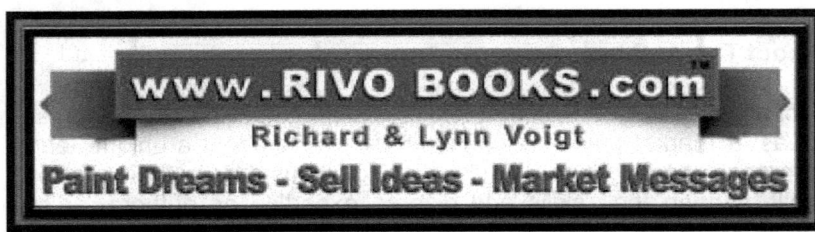

Visit Lynn's Garden: www.WisconsinGarden.com
  view hundreds of great garden video blogs Tips

See Richard's Unique Artwork: www.RIVOart.com
  view over 3,000 original Fine-Art compositions

Our Book Titles Now Available On Amazon:

THE GOLDEN VAULT OF MOTIVATIONAL QUOTATIONS
Words of Wisdom from The Greatest Minds & Leaders

BABY NAME .ME - 21,400 Names & Nicknames
For Family, Friends, Pets, Natural & Man-Objects

DOODLE DESIGNS Volumes 1-3
For Professionals & Kids Of All Ages
DOODLE DESIGNS – Vol. 1
DOODLE DESIGNS – Vol. 2
DOODLE DESIGNS Coloring Book Vol. 3

Work MORE Accomplish LESS Get FIRED!

ACTION HEADLINES That Drive Emotions – Volumes 1- 6
 Paint Dreams, Sell Ideas & Market Your Message
Action Headlines That Drive Emotions Vol. 1
Action Headlines That Drive Emotions Vol. 2
Action Headlines That Drive Emotions Vol. 3
Action Headlines That Drive Emotions Vol. 4
Action Headlines That Drive Emotions Vol. 5
Action Headlines That Drive Emotions Vol. 6

IDIOMS – IDIOMS - IDIOMS
6,450 Popular Expressions That Put Words In Your Mouth

The CLICHÉ BIBLE - 8,400 Clichés For Sports Fanatics
& Lovers Of Popular Expressions

MORE THAN WORDS
5000+ Marketing Phrases That Sell

HYPNOTIC PHRASING

WARNING-This Book Teaches You How To Grab Eyeballs

YOUR RIGHT TO WEALTH
Becoming Wealthy Isn't Hard When You Know How

WI GARDEN – Let's Get Dirty
Our Wisconsin Garden Guide Promoting Delicious, Healthier Home-Grown
Fresh Food, With Tools, Tips, & Ideas That Inspire Gardeners!

MONETIZE YOUR SOCIAL LIFE
Earn Extra Income While Having Fun Online

BABY NAMES
21,400 Unique Baby Names & Nicknames

FUNNY HEADLINES vol. 1
3,500 Outrageous Silly Brain Toots

FUNNY HEADLINES vol. 2
3,500 Outrageous Silly Brain Toots

JOBS
10,240 Career Paths That Can Change Your Life!

MONEY WORDS
Powerful Phrases That Million Dollar Copywriters Use To Make Piles Of
Cash On Demand!

GARDEN QUOTATIONS
400 Garden Quotes From The Earth To Your Soul

HEADLINE STARTERS
175,000 Words That Paint Dreams, Sell Ideas, And Market Your Message

BABY NAMES
25,350 Baby Names & Nicknames For Your Family Friends & Pets
    697 pages 7,000 Names with Origin & Meaning plus Top 100 Names,
    And 2,000 Most Popular Names

CURIOUS WORDS
15,800 Words That Expand Your Mind And Change Your Life

INSPIRING THOUGHTS
That Inspire Happiness, Success & A Clearer Understanding Of Life

MARKETING EYEBALLS
100 Ideas That Can Add Unlimited Subscribers To Your Lists

SECOND OF FIVE
My Early Years- From Birth To High School

POWER PHRASES – Individual Volumes 1 - 10
500 Power Phrases That Trigger Greater Profits

POWER PHRASES Pro Edition – Volumes 1-10 (Complete Series)
5000 Power Phrases That Trigger Greater Profits

COMING SOON! – BE THE FIRST TO GRAB YOUR PRO COPY

POWER PHRASES Pro Edition Volumes 1-10 (Complete Series)
5000 Power Phrases That Trigger Greater Profits

What do Marketing Millionaires know that you don't? They know how to pull money out of thin air by using their secret language of Power Phrases.

This Pro Edition of 5000 Red Hot Power Phrases not only saves you time and money but will help jump-start your creative brain in ways you may have never considered. Simply open this amazing collection to any page and find your perfect power phrase. All it may take is simply adding or replacing ONE word. It's simple, quick, and easy!

1. **Want to create more powerful profitable campaign offers?**
2. **Thinking of revitalizing a more professional business identity?**
3. **Want to update old product or service media advertisements?**
4. **Searching for fresh ideas that could improve sales and profits?**
5. **Looking for brand new ways to create stronger media sales copy?**
6. **Ready to use millionaire strategies advancing you to the next level?**

5000 POWER PHRASES is exclusively for professional Internet Marketers, authors,advertisers, executives, business owners, TV & radio reporters, entrepreneurs, administrators, managers, supervisors, teachers and students who want to find and access unique phrases for marketing slogans, presentation bullet points, and interview sound bites that powerfully paint dreams, sell ideas, and market your message.

Stop wasting valuable time, money, and energy racking your brain for new ideas. Create more profitable power phrase marketing campaigns for all your products, services, slogans, bullet points, and interview sound bites that finally grab and hold people's attention and trigger greater profits?

You now have a very powerful and professional marketing tool in your hand. We are confident that you know how to use it wisely in order to maximize the potential of all your marketing campaigns! Lynn and I **Thank You** for your support and purchase.

CLAIM 500 MORE POWER PHRASES!

Thank you for purchasing this eBook and in doing so we would like to send you **500 More Red Hot Power Phrases for FREE!**

When you post a **positive review of this Book on Amazon Books** under this title you'll receive an additional **500 POWER PHRASES**. Your review may also be sent directly to us.

Your request must be received within 30-days of purchase. Once your positive Book review is posted and verified, simply email the following to **(500@RIVOinc.com)**:

1. Full Name of Purchaser
2. Email address
3. Paypal Invoice Number
4. Copy of your posted Book Review*

Once we receive the above, we'll send you 500 Power Phrases **(PDF)** emailed to the address you provided.

Visit: www.RIVObooks.com for additional volumes as they become available including the Pro Edition of 5000 Red Hot Power Phrases that say what you mean to say and trigger greater profits.

Lynn and I look forward to your written comments and suggestions as we love hearing from each of our readers.

Richard & Lynn Voigt
RIVO Inc – RIVO Marketing
13720 West Keefe Avenue
Brookfield, Wisconsin 53005 USA
Telephone: (262) 783-5335
www.RIVObooks.com

P. S. If you love gardening, catch us on www.WisconsinGarden.com

*NOTE: This offer is valid providing it does not violate the terms of service of the entity with whom you made this purchase. Duplicate or incomplete entries will also not be eligible and this offer is limited to one request per email address. All eligible review submissions become the property of RIVO Inc - RIVO Marketing – RIVO books and may be used as promotional testimonials ads on RIVO Inc websites. This offer may be withdrawn at any time without prior written notice.

www.ingramcontent.com/pod-product-compliance
Lightning Source LLC
Chambersburg PA
CBHW060709280326
41933CB00012B/2363

* 9 7 8 1 9 4 0 9 6 1 0 4 0 *